Computer Maintenance Hacks

Computer Maintenance Hacks

Computer Maintenance Hacks

15 Simple Practical Hacks to Optimize, Speed Up and Make Computer Faster

Life 'n' Hack

ISBN 978-1-548-86618-1

Printed in the United States of America

First Edition

KEYS

Computer Maintenance Hacks

INFO INTRO:

System Operation Commence

As most of you probably know, taking care of your computer is as important as maintaining your car.

Over the lifetime of an owned computer, many of us will get lazy and seldom run the antivirus/optimizer of choice - except when it pops up to remind us that we have it, or when the computer gets slow and we remember we have those tools at our disposal.

But the truth is that one should clean their computer, no matter the operating system, *regularly*.

Why? Well, to start, regularly maintaining your computer has its pros. It helps to:

- Maintain the speed, performance, and efficiency of your computer and provide a pleasant experience while working with this tool.

- Keep your personal information, such as your dozens of login combinations; your SSN; your ID number; your bank information; etc., safe from cyber criminals.

Computer maintenance is more than just keeping your computer running fast, it also keeps your data safe from would-be thieves and protects your computer from all sorts of malware. This is true even for those of you who wait until the last minute to clean it or neglect to implement the proper precautionary measures after your system has already been affected by the damage.

Hence, maintaining your PC or Mac is vital to ensuring a long life span for the computer. After all, every computer will eventually slow down in time - be it from running loads of programs or as a result of something more malicious.

QUESTIONNAIRE: Regardless of your operating system preference, pick the answers that most match your computer usage behavior.

1. How often do you empty your recycle bin?

a.) Once a week.

b.) When it is completely full.

c.) What's the recycling bin?

2. How often do you remember to install updates on your computer?

a.) As soon as you are notified to do so.

b.) When you receive a message about the programs being way outdated.

c.) You don't remember.

3. Why do you think your computer is running slowly?

a.) There are too many programs running at the same time.

b.) Possibly because of a virus.

c.) You have no idea. All you know is that you have to solve this problem.

4. How seriously do you handle your passwords?

a.) Very seriously.

b.) You use them but tend to lose track of them.

c.) You don't give much thought when creating them and even share them with others.

- If you've mostly picked "a," then you are very cautious with your computer. You have all the software and programs necessary to keep your machine up to date and working as you expect it to. What you need to do now is gain more insight to improve your computer maintenance.

- If you've mostly picked "b," you are aware of how tricky computers can be, but you either don't have enough time to come up with a plan to take care of your computer or you are simply overwhelmed by all the steps you have to follow in each task. Hopefully, you will gain much more experience to keep your PC running for years to come.

- If you've mostly picked "c," then you are probably reckless when it comes to taking care of your computer. You, grasshopper, must continue onward to discover the steps you can take to protect and prevent any harm to your system.

HACK #1:

Protect Computer with Antivirus and Anti-Malware Software

Before we get into this, it cannot be stressed enough that you should be backing up your data regularly. Whether it be via a cloud service, a physical external hard disk, or both...**BACK UP YOUR DATA!**

Many of the following steps will remove files from your computer, and while they'll largely be unnecessary and worth removing, no program is perfect. Now that is out of the way, let's get down to the process of improving your system's performance and security.

Having your computer hacked or invaded by viruses is no fun. It slows down your computer and can even infect your files or a number of programs you use every day, opening you up to possible data loss.

Misconception: Although the general belief out there is that Mac computers are more solid and free from cyber-attacks, Mac owners can still face problems as there are a few substantial cases where Macs have ended up horribly infected.

The best way to prevent this is to do something basic, which is to install antivirus combined with an anti-malware (and you don't necessarily need to pay anything).

This is what you need to do:

1. Install a free version of the most recommended antivirus software by typing "best free antivirus for Windows (the current year)" or "best free antivirus for Mac (the current year)." The list is long, but the most popular ones for PCs are Norton, McAfee, Avast, TotalAV, Scanguard, and Kaspersky. Some of these

programs offer advanced features for an annual fee, but the basic features are often free. For most users, these will be sufficient.

2. Now install an anti-malware. There are several ones available for free, but before you pick any one of them, check for reviews by typing "PC free anti-malware" or "Free anti-malware for Mac," and pick the one with the highest rating (which is normally the first one on the list). Some of the most reputed anti-malware for both PCs and Mac computers are Malwarebytes and BullGuard.

3. As you now have both installed, use your antivirus to do a first scan, and then launch the anti-malware too. If there's any virus or other threats found that can slow your computer down, allow the antivirus or anti-malware to delete them permanently, by clicking on that option (the antivirus usually gives you the option to simply quarantine them).

4. After each scan, restart your computer (PC or Mac). This ensures that harmful programs and files are fully removed and refreshes your computer to make it run optimally again. Many of these programs will tell you to restart anyway if you forget to do so after the scans conclude.

Note: If not already setup to do so, most of these programs offer a free service to automatically remind you or even automatically run their scans to keep your computer clean - even if you're doing some other task or logged off the computer. This is a great option to let us be lazy and still be secure in the knowledge that our computer is at least minimally protected.

Having both an antivirus and anti-malware work like a Roman battle formation where one offensive line is protected by another with armors, and they both advance together to face the enemy. In other words, the antivirus and the anti-malware are working together with the antivirus striking first, and then its action is reinforced by an anti-malware as they both fight the similar threats together.

ASSIGNMENT: Now, it's your turn to install your antivirus and anti-malware. It's important (in the long term) to look for one that offers live-scanning of your computer. These programs often offer to scan your computer when you request or even schedule it to run automatically; make sure they scan downloads/links/etc. as you receive them, otherwise you are simply responding to the threat, not preventing it.

HACK #2:

Optimize Computer to Speed It Up

There are software aimed at optimizing your computer, simply known as "optimizers," which scan and clean your computer plus help you get rid of unnecessary documents, allowing your computer to run at optimal performance.

This is how you should approach them:

1. Avoid optimizers that come with options/features that have nothing to do with maintenance (like offering weather services or numbers to call in case there is a problem) because they will only crowd your computer's capacity and slow it down. All too often these are simply viruses pretending to be legitimate software.

2. Do a web search of "effective computer optimizer reviews for PC" or "effective computer optimizer for Mac" (granted, Mac computers have fewer problems than PCs, so you might not need to install one). Here's a list of recommended optimizers*:

- **For PCs:** Easy PC Optimizer, IObit Advanced SystemCare, and Piriform CCleaner.

- **For Macs:** CleanMyMac2, MacKeeper, and Gemini.

*Remember, the top ranking spot changes every year so be sure to do your homework each year.

3. Read the reviews and judge for yourself. What matters is that you get the services you need in one of these optimizers, even if it doesn't have the number one rating ("Do I need X or Y for my PC?"). Take your time to draw your own conclusions, paying attention to each optimizer (in terms of features you need).

4. Download the optimizer you've selected (preferably a free version, so that you can have time to judge the effectiveness of the software). Reasons for downloading an optimizer could differ, meaning that your Mac computer might be saturated with files or software you are not using, or your PC might have slowed down because of its age. Regardless, you can now solve many of these issues by running your optimizer while you are using your computer or after you are done; the choice is yours. The optimizer will scan your computer, get rid of unnecessary files, defragment the disk, and boost your computer's performance.

Note: If you choose to use a feature to clean up your computer and its files, make sure to take the time to go through and tell the software what you want to keep. It may believe that a file you downloaded is worthless, causing you to lose hours of work or worse.

5. One last advice is to always restart your computer after using the appropriate options offered by your PC

or Mac optimizer. This will help finalize the actions taken by the software (whether it is to erase files or to quarantine a number of files). After you've restarted your computer, you should feel the difference in terms of speed.

6. After your trial period, you can now decide to upgrade your current computer optimizer or perhaps skip to another one. There's no harm in trying out several optimizer services but as with any program, this can lead to clutter with each one installing every necessary file needed to run.

ASSIGNMENT: Look for the ideal optimizer by visiting a review site on Google. Remember to read all the reviews (perhaps two or three reviews per application), and then form your own judgment about the optimizer that might work best for you. After installation, run the application and see the difference between having an optimizer and not having one. Remember, these applications are sometimes made by independent developers and many developers will offer the program as a trial with or without telling you, forcing you to use only one or two features or pay a fee to buy the full program. However, some programs truly are free. Just keep at it to find one you like that you don't have to bankrupt yourself to get.

HACK #3:

Run Disk Utility to Fix Errors

As soon as you go through a series of file system errors, it will become clear that, over time, disk maintenance is necessary. (This is true for both Mac and PC; it's inherent to how we store data.)

One way to achieve this end is to run the utility disk for both Mac and PC.

Here's how it's done for both:

For Mac:

As previously mentioned, Mac computers have the privilege of being less vulnerable to hacking, but that does not mean that they can't run low on disk space or that they don't need a maintenance regimen.

1. After you've chosen the Apple menu and restarted your Mac, go to your Application/Utilities folder.

2. As you hear the Startup chime, hold down the Command and "R" keys at the same time.

3. Select the disk you wish to repair.

4. Click on your first aid tab, where you will find the next procedures to follow. Click "Run." If there are no problems or the problem has been solved, you will be notified.

5. On the other hand, if the file is still corrupted you will have to back up your disk because it means it needs to be reformatted. After reformatting your disk, reinstall MacOS, and you can now restore your backed-

up data. This is an extreme measure but will fix the issue.

For PC:

In Windows there is a utility called "CHKDSK," which is Windows' utility used to check the integrity of the hard disk on your computer. So, as we did for Mac, let's go through this maintenance process, this time for PC:

1. Begin by booting your computer and going to "My Computer."

2. Right click on the hard drive on which you wish to run the utility, then click on Properties.

3. Click on "Tools," then you will see the "Error Checking" tab appear. Select "Check Now."

4. In order to run the utility in the "Read Only Mode," click "Start."

5. Repair errors by selecting the "Fix File System Errors" box. Click "Start" or select the "Scan" option to attempt recovery of these bad sectors. Then, click "Start".

<u>ASSIGNMENT</u>: Try doing this yourself by following these guidelines, and remember to always **backup your files,** so you don't lose them in the future.

HACK #4:

Stay Up-To-Date on Operating System

Updating applications can save you from all the annoyance and stress that come with having a slow computer. If you don't believe so, just ask all the folks are who are constantly working on their computer and rely on it 24/7...heck, you might even be one of them.

The web is a complex network where everything constantly changes, including new threats to current applications we use daily.

Follow these steps to keep your applications running like new and safe from ever-evolving threats.

If you own a Mac:

1. Open the Application Store on your computer, and click "Updates" on your Toolbar.

2. You will then see which applications need to be updated (the application lets you know which ones are available).

3. If updates are available, click the Update button so that newer versions of the applications can be downloaded and installed.

4. If you don't have an Application Store on your computer, it's not a problem. Simply go to your Apple menu and update your software from there.

If you own a PC:

1.For Windows 10, all updates are automatic, but for all versions prior to Windows 10, you have to open the

Control Panel and click on the "System and Security" or "Windows Update" option, depending on the version of Windows you're running.

2. Windows Update will check for all available updates for your machine. When they are available, all you need to do is to click Install. Note that updates that depend on other updates will always be installed first. There will be some updates that are optional; in fact, most of them are. However, unless you *really* know what you're doing and have a *really* good reason not to, it's best to let Windows update everything.

To keep up with the speed of change on the web or when it comes to innovations in software, check for updates every week. If necessary, write it down on a Post-it or set it as a reminder in your virtual organizer (on your computer or smartphone in the form of notebooks, calendars, etc.).

ASSIGNMENT: From now on, instead of letting your computer alert you about updates that you will ignore (because you don't know if they are real updates or simply "phishing messages" disguised as legitimate updates), follow these guidelines to do it properly yourself by learning how to navigate through your computer to check for available updates.

HACK #5:

Override the Fake Virus Infection Pop-up Annoyance

Have you ever had incidents where you were in the middle of an important assignment, watching an interesting video, or downloading a file, and you received an annoying message alerting you to call a certain number because your computer was infected with a very dangerous virus?

What's even more annoying? You try to close the pop-up or run your antivirus right away, but you can't do anything.

We've all been through that, and it's critical that you know what to do:

1. Ignore the pop-up message or new tab. *It is a scam!* Do not pay any attention to messages saying anything like "Your computer has been infected!" They're just trying to lure you to download their virus.

2. The proceeding steps may cause a loss of data, so, if you can, *save your files* now if you are working on any.

3. If you can close the pop-up or new tab completely, close the application you were previously in at once and immediately run your antivirus. If you have the option, go for a quick scan (the faster, more shallow option), then do a "deep" scan that will cover all your files but takes more time.

4. If you're unable to escape the pop-up message in any way, try holding either "CTRL+F4" or "ALT+F4" on the keyboard to close the browser on PC or "Command+W" if you're on a Mac.

5. If that doesn't work, perform a hard shut down of the computer. Press and hold the "Power" button, and it will shut your computer down completely.

WARNING: *This is the last and final resort.* In cases where the "fake virus message" blocks any possibility of closing the page and you have exhausted every option, requiring a quick emergency shut down (for instance, you're currently being hacked), unplug the power cord or battery. ***Do this only at your own risk!***

6. Restart your computer in Safe Mode. This limits what can run in the background, but you can run most programs in safety even if your computer gets infected. It normally restarts without problems, but the screen usually looks different.

7. As you reach your desktop, run your antivirus software to detect any attack, followed by your anti-malware. Let them quarantine or delete suspicious files and viruses.

8. Restart your computer one more time to restore the Normal Mode.

When this is all said and done, it's best to avoid that site you were previously visiting, as it might not be a protected site making it vulnerable to cyber-attacks.

Keep your antivirus and anti-malware definitions active, so you don't get this type of interruption again. For the vast majority of malware, an outdated antivirus program is as bad as not having one at all.

Mac-only options:

These problems (the correct term is "tech support scam pop-ups") usually occur for PC owners; however, more and more Mac owners are seeing these messages with the same consequences. Users can't close the browser, and thus can't use the computer as though their screen has been frozen.

There are two options here:

Option A:

You can choose "Force Quit."

Option B:

1. You can also close the browser application by double clicking the "Home" button and simply swipe the window down.

2. Delete the browser's history by going to the settings on Safari.

3. The last step would be to relaunch Safari.

ASSIGNMENT: Familiarize yourself with the multiple ways of handling the tech support scam pop-ups for your system.

HACK #6:

Analyze Disk Surface and Repair Bad Disk Sectors

The disk surface of your computer gets damaged after a while, which can slow down its performance to the point where your computer doesn't store data anymore. However, there is a way to detect the status of your disk by using a software that you can download online for free for disk maintenance.

"EaseUS Partition Master" exists for both PC and Mac, identifying bad sectors on your disk by reviewing the hard drive.

For PC and Mac computers:

Go through the following steps to quickly analyze and fix any issue with your storage drives:

1. Download and install "EaseUS Partition Master."

<u>Note</u>: The installation of this program includes settings that automatically download additional software and make changes to some of your search settings. On the "Install Additional Software" page of the installation, make sure to modify the default settings if you don't want to have your default browser changed and additional programs downloaded. The next page asks you for your name and email, both of which you can leave blank.

2. Launch the software.

3. Choose the hard disk you want to surface test, by right clicking the hard disk and selecting "Check Partition."

4. End the process by selecting "Surface Test" which will lead "EaseUS Partition Master" to check bad sectors for the hard disk. All bad sectors will be marked as red.

Disks get automatically fixed after the scan (it's an option given by the software), then it's recommended that you backup all your files to another disk. This is done for several reasons, but mainly for the purposes of keeping a useable backup saved to roll back to if your data gets corrupted.

ASSIGNMENT: See if your disk has any problem. Download/Install "EaseUS Partition Master," and let it scan your disk for anomalies.

HACK #7:

Clean Up the Browsers for Smoother Surfing

It is important to clean up the browser or browsers you use frequently. Over time every browser accumulates data including your history, cookies, media licenses, etc., and these add up - causing your browser to slow down considerably over time.

The procedure to clean your browser is more or less the same in every browser, but we will go over the top five well-known browsers out there.

For Chrome:

1. Open the Chrome browser.

2. Press Ctrl + H to open the left-side history bar.

3. You will have to delete the browser's history by pressing Ctrl + Shift + Del to open the "Clear Browsing Data Window." On this window click the dropdown box to select "the beginning of time" if it's not already selected.

- If you have some auto-fill data saved, such as web addresses or credit card numbers, you can leave that unchecked to keep those.

- The same goes for passwords; if you clear your saved passwords you could lose access to sites if you forget your login information.

4. Click the "Clear browsing data" button.

For Firefox:

1. Open the Firefox browser.

2. Go to the very top menu bar and click History > Clear Recent History.

3. A pop-up screen will appear. Choose the desired "Time range to clear."

4. Select all data you want to delete.

5. Hit "Clear Now" and you're done.

For Microsoft Edge:

1. Open the Microsoft Edge browser.

2. For clearing the history of your browser, press Ctrl + H to open the history menu.

3. Select "Clear all history" by choosing the appropriate boxes for types of data you'd like to clear.

4. End the process by selecting "Clear."

For Opera:

1. Open the Opera Internet browser.

2. Press Ctrl + H to open the History tab.

3. Move on to deleting history by clicking "Clear browsing data" option.

4. Click the down-arrow and select "the beginning of time."

5. Check the appropriate boxes, then click "Clear browsing data."

For Safari:

1. Open the Safari browser.

2. Open the History menu in the menu bar.

3. After seeing the last 10 listed web pages you have visited, there will also be a menu option for each of the last 6 or 7 days containing the web pages visited during each of those days (Safari only keeps history for the last 7 days).

4. Select "Clear History and Website Data" in the menu (choose how far back you want to delete history, such as the last 60 minutes, today, today and the day before, or all history).

5. Click the "Clear History" button to clear browser history, as well as browser cookies and data.

HACK #8:

Defragment Disk Drive to Boost Performance

When your computer is running a bit slow, you can try to improve its performance by defragmenting it.

For Mac:

The defragging process is automatic through a process known as "Hot File Adaptive Clustering" or HFC; no further action should be required for Mac owners. This is where Apple deserves a standing ovation from the computer community. *Hats off!*

For PC:

Your files can also get defragged automatically (if set by default), but it is not done consistently, so you can still experience issues such as slow loading times. As such, to defrag your (mechanical) disk you will have to:

1. Open the disk optimization tool by searching for "optimize" or "defrag" in the taskbar.

2. Select your hard drive and click "Analyze" (for an SSD, or solid-state drive, this option doesn't exist).

3. You can check the percentage of fragmented files in the results.

4. Begin the actual defragmenting process by clicking "Optimize." Make sure you don't need your computer for the next few hours and let Windows defragment the drive. This may take a while. If the program asks you to restart the PC after completion, do so.

If you're using a PC, you should defragment monthly, or more often if you use your computer extensively. It's worth noting how fast the computer is before and after you defragment your drive(s) to determine if you need to run the process more often or if it's ok to wait longer before defragmenting again.

HACK #9:

Shut Off Hidden Programs Running in Background

Do you ever feel like a spoiled kid because you have so many cool programs on your computer?

We all know how that feels; however, we also know that having to wait ten minutes for your computer to load is rather irritating.

Surely you must have those moments when you just have to get to work immediately, but you feel sabotaged by your machine because you can't seem to get anywhere until X and Y browsers are launched or until A and B programs are opened...sluggishly waiting.

What's the culprit? There are background programs that slow your computer down and drive every computer user insane.

How do you treat this insanity?

For PC owners:

1. Go to "Start" and click "Run".

2. Type "MSCONFIG" in the search window at the bottom of the Start Menu. This will launch Microsoft's System Configuration Utility.

3. Click on the Startup tab. It will take you to a page with a list of programs that start when you boot your computer; uncheck those that you aren't using or don't need. The list of programs that you should keep active includes ScanRegistry, TaskMonitor, SystemTray, and LoadPowerProfile. They need to be running all the time in order for your computer to work properly.

4. Carry on by click on the "OK' button. A message will appear where you will be told to restart your computer to finalize your changes. Click on "Yes" to restart your computer.

It's worth noting that not all of these running processes are bad. For instance, the Chrome browser runs what appears to be many versions of itself during operation but this is normal. Unless you know what you're disabling, it's often best to leave it be. You could accidentally disable or end a process that the computer needs to operate. Stick to programs you recognize and you should be in good hands.

For Mac owners:

You must be logged on as an administrator throughout the process.

1. Begin the process by launching the Activity Monitor application by entering the first few letters of its name into a Spotlight search. Select it in the results at the top.

2. Select the CPU tab of the Activity Monitor window, and select all the processes from the menu bar, as they come.

3. Click the heading of the % CPU column in the process table to sort the entries by CPU usage.

4. You will have to post values for % User, % System, and % Idle at the bottom of the window.

5. Carry on by selecting the System Memory tab. Pay attention to the values showing at the bottom of the window.

6. Select the Disk Activity tab. Post the approximate values shown for Reads in/sec and Writes out/sec.

7. Launch the Console application in the same way you launched Activity Monitor and select All Messages from the SYSTEM LOG QUERIES menu on the left. (Go to "View" > "Show Log List" if you don't see all messages on the menu bar).

8. Now select the 50 most recent entries in the log.

9. Copy these entries to the Clipboard (Command + C).

10. Paste into a reply to this message (Command + V).

Note that when posting a note, you should be brief and post only what is requested and to always anonymize before posting.

ASSIGNMENT: Whether you own a PC or a Mac computer, it's worth your time to evaluate why a program is running. If you have any doubt, all you need to do is run a search online for the name of the program to find out if you should keep it running because some programs may be critical to your system's operation.

HACK #10:

Restart Computer to Avoid Memory Leak

The list of guidelines in order to avoid memory leak for your computer is neither long nor difficult to follow.

All you'll need to do is periodically restart your PC or Mac, which will free up RAM; help purge your computer's virtual-memory swap files; and, last but not least, help regenerate some cache files.

The common reasons why your computer needs to be rebooted/restarted are numerous, but important: A computer that constantly slows down or freezes takes a toll on your hardware and can lead to the blue screen of death (the blue-screen error message page when your system crashes).

All you need to do is shut down your computer at night or when you know you won't be using your Mac or PC. This will fix your computer most of the time. Think of it as a daily cleanse.

Please note that while it does help to refresh your system to restart it (for instance, after uninstalling programs), it is detrimental to your power supply to frequently restart your computer. Once a day is fine, but, in the long run, it does not help your computer if you restart it multiple times a day.

HACK #11:

Relaunch Web Browsers to Limit RAM Demand

Another hack that can help maintain a healthy computer is to simply close and relaunch your browser(s). This can free up a lot of cached memory for your computer and often aids in the browser's performance.

In most modern browsers you can even choose to have the browser save the session you were previously running. This makes the pages you have open when you close the browser reopen immediately when you restart it.

Now, assuming you choose to not use this feature:

1. Close your browser after finishing any unsaved work you have completed.

2. Relaunch your browser.

3. Go to "History" to reopen all the windows you were on before you decided to close your browser.

4. Repeat this process every time you start seeing your browser(s) slowing down (perhaps twice a day, or twice weekly depending on how much you use your computer).

Short as they may be, following these simple instructions will significantly boost your computer's performance by keeping an often-critical program running at peak performance.

HACK #12:

Dust the Hardware to Prevent Overheating

Now don't worry, dusting does not require you to remove sensitive parts off your computer.

It simply serves to prevent dust from building up over time by blowing pressurized air through your computer's hardware (including the laptop's accessible parts) with a pressurized air can made specially for computers. It is highly suggested that you buy one of these cans, available for around $10 for a two-pack online or from a big-box store, as they'll do a much better job than the human mouth will ever do at getting into tiny crevices between parts.

Now, why would you want to clear the dust off your computer's parts? Well, letting it build up can cause some big problems:

- It often causes your computer to heat up excessively.

- It can cause your computer to slow down or become unresponsive (just like viruses and malware tend to do).

- It can cause your computer to shut off.

- It can cause Windows (if you own a PC) to display the blue screen of death.

While you don't have to become an expert on the hardware of your system to clear out any dust, you will have to "crack open" the tower.

Note: This is not a step a user of an all-in-one or a laptop system should ever do without the assistance of a repair technician. You can, and likely will, damage parts if you try to force your way into a system in a manner not designed to be undertaken.

That warning aside, in most cases it's not a big deal to open up a tower. Just go onto YouTube and search for your tower model and there will be many videos that come up showing you how to safely and easily remove the side of the case.

Once you get the case open, clear any dust from the following areas:

- Air intake fans
- Air exhaust fans
- CPU
- Heatsinks
- RAM
- Empty expansion slots
- And any other hardware components your system has

Outside of the tower, it's useful to clear out your keyboard too. This varies somewhat depending on your choice for keyboard but most have large, raised keys which can trap food particles and dust over time, possibly leading to corrosion of the parts or at least a dirty keyboard.

If going through this step has you thinking that it's far beyond your skill level, then rest assured. It isn't a difficult process. Take your time to do a thorough job cleaning all the internal parts and you'll be fine.

ASSIGNMENT: Try to apply this maintenance regimen for your computer at least once every 6 months or once every 12 months, depending on the type of environment you live in (dusty or moderately dusty). Most especially if the computer system is running in a house with people who smoke, the user will often have to clean out the hardware every 3 months or so to keep it up to the same standard as a non-smoking home.

HACK #13:

Store Files in Backup Drives to Free Up Space

Have you ever felt like your computer was a mess? That you couldn't erase a file detected as "corrupt" because you simply didn't recognize it? Have you wasted your time looking all over your computer for a file, having forgotten where you put it?

The best way to deal with this is to invest some time to organize your files, using an external storage medium of your choice.

1. Open the file explorer on your computer where your files currently reside. On this page click "new" as an option, then click "folder." It's best to place this folder

wherever you will remember it. The desktop is a good option to make folders easy to find.

2. Name your folder one of the following ways: pictures, music, work, health, others, bills, etc.

3. Transfer your picture(s) to your picture folder, your work files to your work folder, your bills to your bill folder, etc.

4. Then transfer your files to a USB disk or other storage device by once again right-clicking on each folder and choosing "send to," which gives you several options. Pick the USB flash disk options (or the name you've given your disk). Or simply right-click the folder and select "copy," then right-click "paste" the folder onto the screen for the USB disk. (The transfer should not take too long, depending on the type of files you are transferring; photos, MP3s, and videos are normally the largest and take the longest to transfer.)

5. Once the transfer is done, the same files will still exist on your computer. You will now have the choice to get rid of the ones you don't need anymore. This way your USB disk will become a sort of archive, where you place files you know you will not be working with anytime soon. Make sure these files are well labeled, with dates and other details (if necessary). One way to do this is to have the main folders on your USB or external hard drive be named the archive date, and have the specific work, video, picture, etc. folders within these main folders. This allows you to go back to a specific point in time to see the files you had.

Doing this will help you stay better organized, make quick decisions when your antivirus tells you a file has been corrupted (you know which one it is right away), and it will also help you save up some space in your local disk.

One last piece of advice would be to give a name to your USB disk. You can do so by right-clicking on the USB disk's icon and choose the rename option.

ASSIGNMENT: Your exercise this time will be to properly label your USB flash disk (for example, BradsUSB, Backup, Vacation2015, etc.) Next, create a number of folders that will be labeled (videos, work, bills, etc.). Transfer these files to your USB flash disk to make duplicates of these files. Lastly, complete the process by deleting some of the folders you feel you don't need on your computer. From now on, save most of your files on a USB flash disk to avoid losing them or risking corruption by a virus and to free up space for your computer to run more smoothly.

HACK #14:

Utilize Other Computing Devices to Unburden Computer

Today almost everybody has a smartphone, meaning that you can not only call and talk to people on the phone, but you can also watch movies, play video games, read e-mails, and even work from your phone.

With all these great faculties, why not transfer some of your computer activities onto your smartphone?

- Transition certain functions like reading your emails, using Skype, communicating with clients, and referencing with files on your smartphone. That means you will have to download applications on your phone, such as Skype; Yahoo Mail; or even

Google Sheets, that will allow you to perform these types of tasks.

- You are going have to be resourceful of space on your phone, so as said earlier, get rid of applications you know you will never use.

- Only use your computer to use Microsoft Word or AbiWord (for Mac), which will be more difficult on your smartphone due to its size.

Simply transfer the basic tasks to your smartphone which you need on-going up-to-date access to and notifications as soon as they arrive, like receiving emails, reading the news, communicating on Skype, ordering something online, etc.

For delicate tasks like using Microsoft Word, editing pictures, downloading videos or music, etc., use your actual computer.

This practice will help you not only save up energy on your computer, but it will also help you to avoid overworking it.

ASSIGNMENT: Start transferring your light tasks on your smartphone from now on, like reading and replying to emails, making bids on eBay, consulting your kids' homework from the school's application, etc. Keep the heavy tasks for your computer and start saving energy and preserving your computer for years to come.

HACK #15:

Utilize VPN to Remotely Connect to Workstations Anywhere

Besides using your smartphone to take the load off of overworking your computer, you can use "virtual private network (VPN)" to connect to your main workstation from any computer from anywhere in the world.

Just like how digital media are replacing the need to own DVD and CD players, digital computing is the future - and soon, we may not even need to own a physical computer when all we need to do is access our very own virtual computer out there on a server.

In our growing world of constant connectivity, it's likely that if you work in the business world you have a desktop

PC to do your work with, and perhaps a tablet or other laptop if you travel to compliment that desktop while you travel. These are great tools for you to use, but they have their limitations.

- For example, if you use a laptop as a backup, and not your main computing device, while you travel outside the office you can't access the files on your work hard drive without using a cloud storage solution. These can be useful, for sure, but what if you need to use the PC directly?

The solution is simple, and you may even have used it before in a different way.

A very common tool for IT professionals is to remote-in to your workstation, especially if you have an issue while they're in another building or even another state. This setting is also an option you have at your disposal.

Default on Windows 7 computers is the software necessary to connect a home computer or perhaps a work laptop to your business' internal network. This VPN is used by many people for just as many reasons, ranging from simply wanting more security as they browse the internet, to the business professionals who need to access their computers from elsewhere.

If you're looking to set up a VPN for business purposes:

If you need to connect to a VPN to access work files while you're away from the office, then in all likelihood the IT department has the software available for you to use to achieve this.

Virtually all businesses, in order to maintain a degree of security, have a firewall which would normally block a connection that you attempt to set up yourself, so all you need to do is to talk to IT about the connection.

They'll likely ask to see the computer you want to use remotely. After you supply that, they should have you connected soon. (It's very unlikely a business will allow you to connect to their network, even as an employee, without using proper security protocols, so don't be surprised if they have to install some programs like antivirus or anti-malware to be sure that their network won't be threatened.)

If you're looking to set up a VPN for personal use:

If you want to use a VPN to simply make your browsing more secure at home, for anything from Skype calls to keeping your browser history away from any programs that would track you, the process has, thankfully, gotten much easier over the years.

PC Magazine has listed their top-rated VPN services (search for "PC Magazine best VPN insert current year"), starting with IPVanish VPN, NordVPN, and PureVPN. Of course, these aren't your only choices;

there's plenty of good options aside from just these three, and they all offer similar, but not identical services. Different VPNs will offer some different features, such as allowing P2P and BitTorrent, whereas others boast being able to connect every device your own to your one account.

By and large, the only step you have to undertake to install one of these services is to buy one. You typically purchase a subscription for a year or per month; and once you pay for it, the site will begin the download or send you a link to download the service. From there the program will ask you what settings you want to be customized, that being about the end of the process after you save your settings.

One final note regarding these VPNs, for both business and pleasure: VPNs are not perfect, and they're far more practical for work than for personal use. Plus, they do come with inherent risks; you have to trust that the company hosting your VPN is in no way tracking who you are even as you change IP from one end to the other. This shouldn't make you paranoid, but rather careful about which provider you choose.

Don't go for the cheapest just because you want to save a few bucks. You're better off going with a reputable provider, such as the ones listed on PC Magazine's top VPN list, than a cheaper competitor who may have questionable ethics.

INFO UNLOCKED:

System Optimization Complete

We use computers every day - and for almost everything nowadays. We certainly don't want to waste money buying new ones every year then transfer our entire lives and work to a new computer all over again.

Therefore, regularly perform maintenance on your computer to preserve and keep it in top shape for as long as possible.

Maintaining your computers, no matter brand or operating system, is actually not that difficult when you look at it, but many people still neglect doing it.

Clean up your computer's hard drive by deleting unnecessary files and scanning it at least once a week with antivirus/malware software. You can also opt for a computer optimizer for both your PC and Mac computers.

Always install and get up to date with the latest versions of the programs you use to be compatible with the web and other functionalities out there. Why? Because many hackers like to exploit the loopholes of outdated programs.

Besides keeping your firewall activated to block and get notified about harmful sites and programs, stay informed regarding new computer threats because every year cyber criminals become all the more clever, learning new ways to try to breach your system.

Don't forget that all these practices will not only maintain your computer but also help you safeguard your identity.

Take the time now to start using these practices and you'll ensure computer performance for years to come.

www.ingramcontent.com/pod-product-compliance
Lightning Source LLC
Chambersburg PA
CBHW061028050326
40689CB00012B/2737